AF445871

Birds Flew In

Cover Art by Sarah Yeoman
Book Design by Alan Abrams

ISBN: 979-8-9992568-9-8

Sligo Creek Publishing
9039 Sligo Creek Parkway
Silver Spring, MD 20901
www.sligocreekpublishing.com

Birds Flew In

Poems with birds inside

Roderick Deacey

CONTENTS

Birds flew into these poems, sometimes merely as a mention, sometimes just a feather or two, sometimes swirling and tumbling across the sky for the pure joy of it; here they are: herons, eagles, owls + hoots, ospreys, peregrine falcon, goshawk, red-tailed hawks, red-shouldered hawk, rough-legged hawk, kestrel, sharp-shinned hawk, Cooper's hawk, things with feathers, willow warbler, Mexican macaws, meadowlark, crows, pheasant, Canada geese, hounds of heaven, feathered friends, house finches, goldfinches, parrots, parakeets, seagulls, starlings, big-city hustler pigeons, wood pigeons, small birds, albatross, mockingbird, blue jay, lark, magpie, screech owl, seabirds, corvids, sky riders, moorhen, ravens, mountain chickadee, swans, Charlie Parker, and a few that flew under the radar.

HERONS AWAIT

Poems are like herons
standing like statues in the reeds
as you float down life's river.
If you are lucky, they fly up for you,
to soar into the cageless vault of sky
with grace &, perhaps, beauty—
   which you may capture
     on your smartphone
       for sharing later.

BIRDWATCHING 101—A RAPTOR?

It flew by too fast!
It definitely wasn't an eagle or an owl.
It wasn't an osprey—not black & white,
& no fish, they're always holding a fish.
Perhaps it was a peregrine falcon
but maybe it wasn't quite that fast,
so it had to be one of the hawks.
A goshawk, then, a northern goshawk—
such an excellent name! No, not big enough.
I suppose it may have been a common-or-garden
red-tailed hawk—& isn't there
a red-shouldered hawk? A possibility.
It didn't have feathered legs
so clearly not a rough-legged hawk.
I think it was bigger than a kestrel
which could mean a sharp-shinned hawk
or a Cooper's hawk—I just don't know
what either of those really look like.
How many hawks are there, anyway?

It flew too fast—I was just taking an allergy pill
& I couldn't focus the binoculars in time,
so in reality, it was a hooked-beak brownish blur
zooming past. But I am almost certain
it was a raptor.

SMALL MESSAGES

no burning bush appears for me
no booming voice from the sky
no flute songs from the canyons
no mystery writing on the wall
     in some long-dead language

instead   small messages arrive
locked in dew on the dawn grass
coded scarlet in a feather fallen
from the wing of a Mexican macaw
written carefully on a hop toad's
lumpy skin in invisible ink
     readable only in moonlight

sometimes   sendings are voiced
by the wind   shaping storm-borne snow
into patterns of tiny waves
like sand ripples on a low-tide beach
other times   notes are concealed inside
a meadowlark's song   shimmering down
     from a summer sky

I consider the messages
I hum the melodies
     they seem to mean nothing

but wait
stitch them together
& maybe there is something
something slowly on the move
just below the patchwork surface
     huge   scaly   unstoppable

every so often   I catch the briefest glimpse
     of shining golden claws

RIPPLES RECEDING & A SMALL GREEN GOD

it keeps retreating behind me
   that rich golden sunlight
      on riverbank grass
         on the vivid blue petals of periwinkles
        under the hawthorn bushes
      on the same ever-changing river ripples
   on my skin
tanning quietly

I stare into clear water by the lily pads
   tiny scarlet-finned fish flash past
      reflecting golden light
        from silver scales

it's an empty land now
   just trees birds flowers
      wild things in nature's domain
        with a breeze softly rustling
          narrow willow leaves
        gentle percussion
      for the descending song
   of a lone willow warbler
hidden in the overgrown osiers

the people here have all moved on
   sliding away across the years
      their faces fade
        I can't remember them
      I can't miss them
   but I sense absence
a fleeting feeling of indefinable loss
   soon this too will fall back
      too far to recall
        not a concern

I will simply bring to mind
 somewhere else
some other treasured locale

like that vast southwestern desert
   humming quietly to itself
     with no people to lose
       except myself   entranced
         by the astonishing richness
         of Earth's color palette
         rock   sand   saguaro
         sage   mesquite   agave
         white panicles of yucca piercing
         the towering dome of sky
         mist-blue distances
         night skies of lapis lazuli
         splashed by a myriad of stars

the deep resonance
   of the desert's meditation
     speaks of sacred spaces
       old gods & spirits dreaming
         through the flickering years
           drinking in starlight
             older than time
           & then comes
         that same rich golden sunlight
       washing over rocks & sand
     with the sudden desert dawn
   reflected in the unblinking eye
of a small green being
   overseeing his territory
     disguised as a lizard
       the only god
         still awake

HOPEFUL

A post-rain morning, washed clean, invitingly blank—
tabula rasa—granddaughter & I have sketch pads.
Of late, her seven-year-old self favors houses
while I work at bringing some unsuspecting plant to life
      with pen & ink.

I used to echo the swoops & swirls
of those things with feathers
but never could quite capture
their effortless grace through the air
& I am sadly reminded of their recent relentless decline,
fading almost as fast as their huge scaly forebears.
Can they still embody hope?
      Maybe, Emily, the metaphor is now over-extended.

In North America, we managed to lose three billion birds
in 50 years—that's since the Beatles broke up,
which was only yesterday,
      when all our troubles seemed so far away.

Given the chance, I draw a passable Peace Lily,
readily recognizable.
Granddaughter casually reveals
her "House of the Day."
      Lawdy, Lawdy, Miss Clawdy!
It's an enormous mansion made entirely of flowers!

I can't speak to the structural integrity
of this magnificent floral edifice, but I have to say,
a house of flowers! Such vision!

I do hope
there's space for birds in there.

ALMOST A LOVE POEM

I see my voice
left swirls of rhetoric
by the fireplace

words hide in blooms
of tiger lilies
in the alabaster vase

they leap from shelf
to shelf ascending
the ancient oak bookcase

then bounce inside
the sideboard
on chandelier swing high

some glissaaaaaando
out the window
straight up in the sky

they almost hit
a red-tailed hawk
by chance just flying by

why words took these
convolutions
is not exactly clear

plainly my thoughts
did not reach you
they never made it near

I tried to speak
of love my love
but missed your pearl-pricked ear

RAIN WITH A NAME

The storm spins ropes of rain that drench & chill,
as clouds boom like some cosmic cowboy's gun.
The yew tree's full of crows till squalls are done,
while owls hide in the barn, so rats—keep still!

The Percherons munch oats, no signs of fear,
unmoved by howling wind & lightning zap,
while ponies skitter at each thunderclap.
I shut the stable door—no bolting here.

A pair of labs, good working dogs, ignore
the water pounding on their heads & roust
a pheasant. It leaps up, scrabbles its way

through bushes then—poof! Lost in the downpour.
So much water, the river's rising fast—
as ice caps melt, will we be washed away?

MR TIBBLES TRAINS THE LADY NEXT DOOR

It's time to feed me! You've been told, I'm sure.
You're new at this, so I won't make a fuss
but bear in mind that I'm a carnivore.

There's no meat in that red bag by the door—
just lumps of cardboard sprayed with protein dust—
I need real meat; you understand, I'm sure.

The dog wolfs down that fake stuff; begs for more!
My stomach craves flesh—do you get my gist?
Goes along with being a carnivore.

I don't need ribeye when you hit the store,
I'm fine with liver or the cheaper cuts.
I just need meat, that's crystal clear, for sure.

Or I'll take tuna—I like albacore.
Raw & fresh is best; canned if needs must—
fish makes a nice change for a carnivore.

Wait! You're the one who feeds the birds next door!
I don't hunt birds—I don't like feathers much
so I won't eat your feathered friends. I'm sure
you'll track down meat to please this carnivore!

GEESE RETRO

"Across the margent of the world I fled,
And troubled the gold gateway of the stars…"
~ Francis Thompson: *The Hound of Heaven*

Today, I replaced the small vase
of wildflowers normally on my desk
with a jam jar jammed full
of discarded Canada goose feathers,
collected daily through the summer
from the avian grooming ground by the creek.
Instead of focusing on local wildlife
in well-loved woods & along streams
often visited, season by season,
I felt the need to write of wildness, wilderness,
of strange mountains & the jeweled lakes
of the far north, crystalline in the dawn,
or to laud the lush streams of the Delta
in the deep South winter destination
of our resident flock.

To show proper respect for these expansive vistas
I dug out an almost forgotten, unlabeled bottle of ink,
tucked away at the back of a desk drawer.
Then I turned off the laptop & selected a quill.
I took my penknife & carefully cut a nib shape
in the strong hollow shank of the feather—
which is, of course, what a penknife is actually for.
I found some ancient sheets of writing paper,
dipped my new quill pen into the ink
& began to write of great migratory journeys
with the natural world spread like a tapestry beneath me.
Only when I had filled a page with lyrical prose,
scribed in almost legible copperplate,
did I realize that the ink was neither blue nor black
but, appropriately, a vivid emerald green.

Later, the Cairn terrier & I took
our daily walk along the creek & he decided
that, in the natural order of things,
geese definitely belonged in the water
not foraging on dry land. As one,
the indignant birds launched themselves
into the sky. They swooped & circled,
hurling threats & insults at the small dog
before heading east towards the nearest lake.
They kept up a heated conversation amongst themselves
as they flew away, loudly honking & baying
like a pack of demented foxhounds in full cry.
They demonstrated why these geese are often called
"Hounds of Heaven," ostensibly but mistakenly
prompted by Francis Thompson's poem
"The Hound of Heaven," which is about
something else entirely.

At least one bird was surprised in mid-groom
by the flock's hasty departure—
a single quill feather spiraled down
from way up high in the empty sky,
an addition for my jam jar feather bouquet.
I think it might have been an omen
alerting me to something or other—
but just what, for the moment,
escapes me.

LAST OF WINTER

In the final flick of a winter's tale,
snow plastered the host of daffodils
& you were staring out the window.

"But I haven't been anywhere," you said,
"I've been here all the time."
Not so, we are always tripping along

from womb to bloom, to rattling around
in this crepey skin; dry crusts in a paper sack,
ready to be thrown to the carp in the creek.

Except the murky, muddy water conceals
not spring-roused carp, but a giant snapping turtle—
in fact, it could be turtles all the way down.

Infinite regressions may sometimes distract us
but echoes of ancient mysteries may be found
weaving through our swift, bright years.

They bring us hope despite darkness—
hear the midnight song of the mockingbird,
see sun-gilded daffodils defying winter snow.

GAPS

This mind of mine is somehow full of gaps
& more holes keep appearing night by night—
it isn't just a momentary lapse.

First, names I thought I knew slid out of sight,
then faces didn't match up in my head.
I can't remember things exactly right

but one dawn I was rising from my bed
& I still knew the lives of living things—
so now I use wild creatures' names instead.

Melody girl, her voice as high as harp-strings—
"Lark" she is! "Hippo" is the large old man.
Black-suit guy is "Magpie"—his sorrow stings.

They *are* their names; I'll hold them while I can.
I feel them zapping, synapse to synapse.
When they've faded, I'll be as I began.

I know where I'm going, there are no maps
& this old mind of mine is full of gaps.

ANOTHER DRY DAY

They came with the birds, the bone men,
flitting & skittering through the moss trees,
crawling in the chalk of the hill domes—
old ghosts glowing white in another pale dawn.

They came with tidings
wrapped in the usual hints & rumors.
Mighty Achilles has risen yet again—
even now, he can be found
casually breaking the heads
of a dozen Eastside thugs
with one iron fist. They're falling
like too-ripe fruit, with last night's needles
dingle-dangling from their ropey veins.
He's still limping, apparently—
a likely story.

Meanwhile, we're setting spook-wires
& slander charms on a grey morning.
A circle of willow wands marches
around the perimeter.
Here we go—a severed finger
& a hank of hair—beg the blue jay
for a feather & that should do it.
No entrails today; sorry, boys.
It's a dull day in a barren season.

What do the bone men want?
They want to tag along
when we go over the mountain.

They brought evergreen camo blankets
made from Holm oak leaves,
two wild pigs ready for roasting
& six matched pairs
of Japanese *makume-gani* dirks
for hiding beneath the kilt,
guaranteed to slit even the strongest gizzard.
They relieved a trader of some of his stock
out by the western desert.

Only the dirks might be useful
but I've seen these West Coast blades.
They're too sharp for under the kilt
& too short for sentry work.
So, no, we're not interested.
We're faster on our own.

We'll play the odds & leave before dawn.
The ancestors should be dozing by then—
& don't be saying there are no spirits!
No ghosts means no redemption,
& then we must carry these old wounds
forever into the dark.

Send the bone men on their way.
Give them food but tell them nothing.

It's lunchtime.

SUSURRATION

Dedicated to Flaco, the NYC Eurasian owl,
an escapee from the Central Park Zoo
who died from flying into a building.

It was late afternoon when I checked the sky
for approaching rain or an interesting cloud,
when I heard a susurration of wings,
unseen but not too far away.

I thought at first it might have been
a cloud of house finches, but they're too noisy,
constantly chattering & arguing
amongst themselves,
so it couldn't have been them.

Even the members of our local charm
of goldfinches are too talkative to take off
without chirping, so I would have heard them
announcing their presence together
with the whirr of wings—so not them.

The same can be said of the rainbow pandemonium
of parrots, parakeets & Mexican macaws
released just last week from a local pet store
by protesters against birds being kept in cages.
The escapees have been squawking & talking
in the park ever since, begging for birdseed,
purloining pizza crusts like seagulls on a spree,
& asking, "Who's a pretty boy?"
from high in the sycamore trees.

A murmuration of starlings
would have been too loud
to make the feathery noise I heard
& certainly wouldn't have been unseen,
as their huge wheeling flight formations
can take over the whole sky.
Why do they do that?

Just then, I heard the sound of wings again,
this time with a slight clattering accent!
Aha! I recognized that wing-slapping sound—pigeons!

As soon as I realized the source of the susurration,
I spotted a passel of pigeons close at hand,
perched in their regular spots in the plum trees.
More flew in from back by the bird feeders,
briefly clapping their wings as they took off.
These were not your grimy, big-city hustler pigeons,
but well-fed, fit-looking wood pigeons,
nattily dressed in muted greys with black tails,
& white contrast patches each side of their necks.

What were they doing? Well, they *are* pigeons,
so, like chickens, unpleasant untruths & bad behavior,
they were coming home to roost—that's what they do.
They're famous for it, aren't they!
Especially the "coming home" part.

THE VIBRANT LIFE

We felt a hankering
to be as one with the planet,
to immerse ourselves in Nature,
to feel the vibrant life
that surrounds us,
before it all disappears
from screwed-up weather.

We saw an article online
about this bird sanctuary—
Perfect, we thought!
We like birds!
"Especially roasted," you added.
"Stop it," I said.

We drove out there.
It only took four hours.
There were supposed to be
nine square miles of
beach & estuary,
containing as many as
a hundred thousand birds
at any given time.

The parking lot was empty
except for a twenty-year-old Honda Civic
with two flat tires.

There was a noticeboard
with a map showing four nature trails.
All four led directly to mudflats
in the estuary.
These were dark brown & shiny,
made of real mud
& were stickily impassable.

Some birds were visible
across the mudflats as tiny white blobs.
They were too far away to identify
with our new bird books.

A solitary heron flew over
neck folded back at an impossible angle—
we *have* a heron on our pond at home,
where our latest study shows
herons live exclusively on koi—
at least, ours does.

At this so-called sanctuary,
there was no visitor center,
no gift shop, no souvenirs,
no café, no coffee bar,
no coke machine,
no viewing deck—
there wasn't even anywhere
to sit down.

"About ten miles back
there is an opportunity
to be as one with The Colonel—
just saying," you said.
"As one?"
I thought briefly…
"Hmm—perfect.
Let's go!
Right now!

This place
is for the birds!"

SWEENEY TREED

the trees hold me
branches shield me
havens from the world
I cannot leave

though I can walk again
the curse is done
the days have flickered by
I cannot leave

peppery watercress
sustains me   I need nothing
birds my companions
I cannot leave

it was a fine madness
but the flame burned low
where should I go now
I cannot leave

I am old it seems
stretched too thin
traveling tires me
I cannot leave

bells still disturb me
I cannot listen
I fear the spearpoint
I cannot leave

the trees guard me
small birds sing
I cannot leave
I cannot leave

ELEGY FOR DEAN YOUNG

> *"Some cries never reach us*
> *Even though they're our own.*
> *The best endings are abrupt."*
> ~ Dean Young: Final lines in his last manuscript

We had really hoped your second heart
would carry you much further, yet
it ceased to beat, abruptly ending your torrent of words,

which contained daffodils &, well, everything—herds
of buffalo, moths, an albatross, swarms of bees, a fleet
of tall ships, swans, owl hoots, plus shiny faucets

of hot & cold lust. You thoughtfully included fake fur coats
for the snowmen lining the drive, then drew our attention
to that persistent puddle of antifreeze—so shiny, so green.

We should also mention your monarchs, not of countries,
not of the glen, but those far-fluttering butterflies,
migrating many miles to Mexico & California.

You were a yodeling redwood avalanching through
the evergreen mountains, sliding up & down,
shedding stanzas as you sped along,

but then you slipped quietly away, into darkness.
No, darkness won't hurt you. You told me
darkness never hurt anyone.

Everything may seem empty now, but maybe not—
just listen. Distant waves ring like bells
& sometimes there are stars.

DON'T TRY TO UNDERSTAND   *Beat poem*

*"...the attitude of faith is to let go, and become open to truth,
whatever it might turn out to be."*
*~ Alan Watts: **The Way of Zen***

Don't try to understand
but stand in the night & let the stars
soak in through your skin
let the owl's screech bring you silence
to hear the silver moonlight sing

don't try to understand
but stand on the shore & let the waves
lull you into dream
let the seabirds' sighing call you
to fabled islands in the stream

don't try to understand
but stand in the wood & let the trees
tell leafy legends
of when the world was young & filled
with all that could be imagined

don't try to understand
but stand on high peaks & let the winds
blow all thoughts away
you can ride the fleeting moment
first breath of a newborn day

> *These days, the best minds of our degeneration*
> *are uncertain about the existence of a personal God,*
> *who some white folks believe has a long, white beard*
> *& votes Republican, although this is unlikely*
> *as Jesus clearly leans toward social activism...*

Anyway, He or She is reputed to love us dearly,
& time will tell who is right, when non-believers
are plunged into the fire, or not.
It's at this point that birds fly in; two crows again,
appearing like swirling blown leaves in the blue heavens...
The corvids cartwheel, cavorting fearlessly through the sky
for the pure joy of it—isn't that enough? CAW, CAW.
Shouldn't we all congratulate ourselves on being alive?
However, beyond that, it's recently been established
that the labors of man don't count for a whole lot.
Money & power games rule, but few can play
& they that do constantly cheat & lie—& promise
violence if you challenge them—isn't that the truth?
So, it's best to seek a still point; to strive for serenity
& ignore the crooks & creeps, with their trails of chaos.
Anyway, in these tense times, there's not much news
that changes what people decide to believe,
just the ongoing stuff versus nonsense debates.
But when the stuff is truth, there's no debate, for nonsense
remains nonsense—two & two never make five
no matter how loudly proclaimed—that's true absurdity.
The crooked path of false equivalence leads
down the road to ruin, where, ultimately,
the aforementioned labors of man
are abandoned, dismantled, deconstructed, disassembled,
demolished, disintegrated, eliminated, eroded & erased—
leaving to the crows the open sky,
the perpetually undulating ocean
& the calm, unfinished stones. Ergo: CAW, CAW...

Don't try to understand
but stand in stillness and let things be
set your senses free
feel eagles above   whales below
where endless sky meets endless sea
endless sky   endless sea.

BRISTLECONE

A day hiking a mountain at the eastern edge of Nevada,
I laid hands on the twisted torso of a bristlecone pine.
I closed my eyes to sense the measured pulsing
of its incredible 5,000-year-old life beneath my fingers.
In the moment, a scatter of ravens swirled around
the tree in its rocky terrain, like guardians,
& a mountain chickadee sang softly.

HIGH PLACES

It was the idea of it
that made me climb the tallest willow tree,
to see if I could spy from the highest branches
whatever was feeding my unspoken yearning,
so I could head in that direction when I came down.

Of course, I never saw anything, but I kept on finding
lofty perches where I could scan the blue distances.
Once, from a rugged cliff in the high desert
I saw a pack of coyotes on the track of something
promising, but when I rappelled to the desert floor
they were lost among rocks; gone like ghosts.

The same desert sent the traditionally lonesome cry
of a steam-driven train whistle to distract me,
but I just hunkered down at the edge of town
& waited for a sign, as one does.
Naturally, it began to rain.
Thinking about it, perhaps rain *was* the sign.

After the storm, I felt like familiar fields, & headed for
the Bridge of Sighs—not sad & sinking Venice,
not the honeyed limestone spires of Oxford,
but flat & fenny Cambridge—I considered studying
architecture, to make poetry in bricks & stone,
or possibly glass, steel, & cedar
with contrasting slabs of Welsh slate
as a nod to Dylan Thomas.

In the end, though,
I decided to simply enjoy the vistas
& to make copious notes in the topmost towers
in case a memoir comes over me.

Also, I make sure to take many photos
of the birds gliding & riding the windy sky
before they have all flown away forever
to a more deserving planet,
whose inhabitants
have not broken the weather.

LA LUMIÈRE

Upstream on the river, night does not fall—
instead, it slides out of the riverside willows
& slithers across the ripples,
mingling with tendrils of evening mist
to cloak the opposite bank in shadow.
In minutes, the dark has swallowed up
the purple willowherb & yellow flag irises.
The last *cuk-cuk-cuk* of a moorhen scurrying
into the rushes joins other nighttime noises,
small nocturnal animals foraging, owl hoots,
& reeds rustling, as the river flows on, unperturbed.

Downstream, the next day is sunny in the morning
but overcast in the afternoon with light rain…
The evening is misty again; night lurks in wait
in the city wharves, warehouses & loading docks,
ready to make its foray across the current.
Soon, its creeping pall envelops all, draining the color
from the red & yellow ochre hulls of boats
& sailing barges & turning rusty-red sails black.
The evening is cool, with the smell of smoke
curling through the air from barge woodstoves.
Lights from the streets & around the docks reflect
on the moving water's surface, giving it
a shimmering silvery presence in the darkness,
& making the serpentine stream seem alive—

"Mais oui—c'est la lumière! Toujours la lumière,"
says Claude Monet, as he cleans his brushes,
puts away his paints & folds up his easel.
"La lumière change tout le temps, tout le temps."
He carefully packs onto his small cart
the eight canvases he has worked on during the day,
all of Waterloo Bridge; he would paint forty-one
at different times, each capturing a different light.
He walks off to his hotel in the dark.

BIRD LIVES!

> *"If you don't live it, it won't come out your horn."*
> ~ Charlie Parker

The city has a long memory—
& honors its shifting alliances,
wearing its tattoos proudly.
Check out the grimy, layered strata
of its ancient, storied underbelly—
those cracked subway walls, the dark
& narrow alleys leading nowhere,
the secret concrete underpasses
crumbling under the weight of years.

Then, if you slide past Keith Haring's
faded dancing men & barking dogs,
past Jean-Michel Basquiat's colorful scrawls
& enigmatic epigraphs,
down where the mortal denizens
of the city night come out to play,
you might just discover
over the top of an old brick archway,
boldly painted in black letters
on a white background—BIRD LIVES!

Bird still lives!

Bebop-a-diddleybop-a-bebop-BOW!

Don't that beat all!

© Copyright Anne Burgess Photo has been altered for black and white printing.

ACKNOWLEDGEMENTS:

*Herons Await, The Last of Winter, Birdwatching 101—A Raptor?,
Mr Tibbles Trains the Lady Next Door, Last of Winter,* and *Elegy
for Dean Young* appeared in *Pen in Hand*, the literary journal of
the Maryland Writers' Association.
Don't Try to Understand appeared in *neo-beatery ballads:
New Beat Poetry* and in the *New Generation Beats Anthology*.

My thanks go to the Ginkgoes: Claudia Gary, Betsey Houghton,
Ruth Holzer, and Susan MacLean, for their help and patience.